THE YEAR OF
IDENTITY
who I know I am

jesuscentricmind.com

The Year of Identity
who I know I am

ISBN: 979-8-9897831-0-6

Jesus Centric Mind Ministries a ministry
of Net-Works Church Laguna Beach

DEDICATION

God, Jesus, and Holy Spirit.

Our wonderful, loving, and supportive parents; Ken & Amy Moyer and David & Renée Lohrke.

Our kids; Lu Lu, Kitty Kat, Sweet Pea, Kademan, and Kolbert...may you relentlessly seek and live into the truth of who you are in Jesus.

Every person God has put in our lives for the purpose of shaping our desires to be missionaries wherever we are and cultivate the ways God works through us.

Everyone who continues to stand in their Spirit with Jesus through the full spectrum of emotional challenges while remembering who they really are.

Prayer Warriors, Jesus Lovers, Church Leaders, Bible Teachers, Uncompromising Truth Seekers, Missionaries, Believers, Disciples, and You

Name ________________________________

Year ________________________________

A MESSAGE FROM US

Thank you for being curious enough to follow the leading of Holy Spirit in discovering more ways to remember your true identity!

The approach at Jesus Centric Mind Ministries is to share with the world the understanding Holy Spirit reveals to and impresses upon our hearts, tested and verified with scripture, the science of renewing the mind, in our own lives, and with clients.

We encourage you to test and verify everything with the Word of God and guidance from Holy Spirit to also know, with conviction, what is true for you.

TABLE OF CONTENTS

WHAT WE BELIEVE

GOD

- There is One True God, eternally existent in three persons, often referred to in the Bible as Father, Son, and Holy Spirit.
- Expressed in all living things, sustaining the testimony of Creator God.
- Is in direct connection and communication with all people through Holy Spirit.
- Revelation of God, Jesus, and Holy Spirit occurs at any moment without limitations.
- Created and Wills to be in Oneness with a united humankind.

JESUS

- God, born as a human with the exact same emotional options as you and all humans.
- Perfectly lived, moment to moment, completely guided by and in compliance with Spirit.
- Modeled living from Spirit Identity, in a human world.
- Through the extremes of His life and death, modeled Oneness with God, and humankind and how to BE Spirit with a human body in a human world.
- Jesus' resurrection shows that He conquered sin and death. Human death is a transition to our eternal existence.
- Ascended to the full presence of God, the Father, the Creator.
- Returns to finish His purpose as Savior, King of Kings and Lord of Lords.

HOLY SPIRIT

- Awakens your conscious awareness and influences your mind to:
  - Remember who you are, as an eternal being.
  - Know you are a creation of God, Elohim.
  - Understand the purpose you have been created as a human.
  - To live from your Spirit Identity as a human in this human world.
  - Learn your eternal purposes.
- Gives you revelatory understanding and acceptance (at the heart level) of God as Jesus, unifying you with God the Father.
- Gives the spiritual gifts of wisdom, understanding, counsel, fortitude, knowledge, piety, and fear of the Lord.
- Witnesses through the Fruits of the Spirit: love, joy, peace, patience, kindness, generosity, faithfulness, gentleness, and self-control.

- Guides you to live as Jesus modeled so that you can be an Extension of God's Love and ultimately ascend to the presence of God.
- Exists omniscient, omnipresent, omnipotent, and eternal.
- Inspired scripture, creates, regenerates, and sanctifies.
- Teaches, guides, comforts, and intercedes.
- Co-equal as one of the three-part deity with God the Father and God the Son while being distinct with a supportive, specific purpose.
- God's mind, spirit, and presence as the inherent guiding intelligence purposed to tabernacle within you and all of humankind.
- Directly accessible presence of God through your subconscious mind without limitations by the Will of God or yourself.

- Gives revelatory understanding of Itself, God, Jesus, God's Word, God's plans, and all of God's creation, at the growth pace of your spiritual maturity.

THE BIBLE

- Inspired by Holy Spirit.
- The authoritative Word of God, Creator of all things.
- When rightly interpreted, aligns with all things that are true and good.

PRAYER

- Communication with God, Jesus, and Holy Spirit.

WHEN ALIGNED WITH GOD'S WILL

- produces knowing the fullness of love, peace, joy, Oneness with God, and humankind.

- Results in revelatory visual, auditory, kinesthetic, and mental understanding.

Strengthens rapport with Holy Spirit.

WHO YOU ARE

We whole-heartedly believe the purpose of this book is to:

- deepen the knowing of who you are as God perfectly designed;
- heighten the sensitivity of your communication with Holy Spirit; and
- powerfully be a resource for your discipleship journey of being more like Jesus every day.

With each page, you are transformed from glory to glory.

We believe people have two identities:

1. Spirit Identity – which is created by God and who now sits in heavenly places with

Jesus upon being born again, at which time their heart and mind awakens to who they really are and they surrender to the supernatural reality and Love of God. (Ephesians 2: 6)

2. Human Identity – which is created by God to live for a span of time on current Earth with free-will in a now sinful-nature reality of God's creation. (James 4:14)

The Hebrew word 'cheder' is used 38 times in scripture to describe the hidden places and secret chambers of the heart (interchangeable with the mind) which can be clouded with sin. Holy Spirit uses emotional discomfort to expose such places for revelatory and supernatural transformation. Jesus Centric Mind Ministries is focused on the reality of this truth throughout the Bible.

Figure 1 illustrates the Drivers of your Mind.

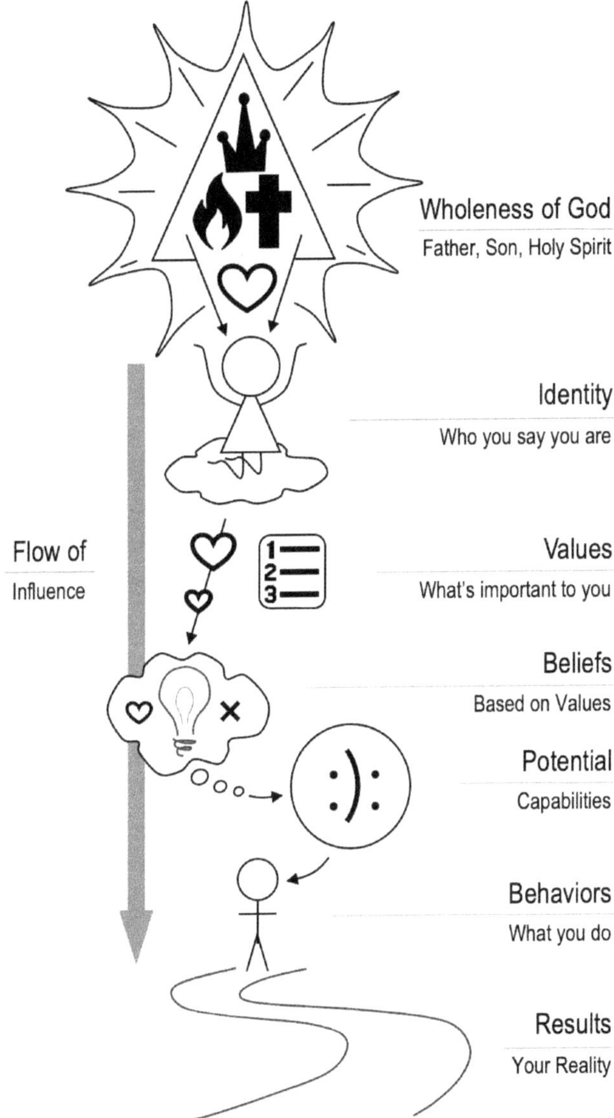

Fig. 1

The renewing of your mind becomes more evident through Parts 1-3 as you meditate on the hundreds of prayerfully selected scriptures from the Bible, be still for what Holy Spirit is communicating to you, and write down the personal revelations as your sacred writing record of discovering supernatural skills, gifts, and fruits.

Part 4 is some of our own personal revelations to edify the experience of awakening and encourage you, as they have encouraged us.

Enjoy this intimate and life transforming LOVE and Identity adventure with:

The One True God - our Creator

The Lord and Savior Jesus – our model

Holy Spirit – Comforter and Guide

SUPERNATURALLY USE THIS BOOK

This is a book of sacred writings…the Bible verses and your journal entries…influenced by God, Jesus, and Holy Spirit. Think of it as a personalized historic, prophetic, and healing record of your revelatory awakenings.

1. Read the daily focus.
2. Prayerfully go into stillness with God and meditate on it.
3. Jot down what comes to your awareness as the meaning Holy Spirit gives you, without judging or editing it in relation to your:
   - thoughts
   - emotions
   - where you feel it in your body

Everything in this book is an expression from you, in your Identity as:

a) An Image Bearer of God, created by God's command; and
b) An Extension of God's Love, chosen by your free-will.

PART 1: IDENTITY-TRANSFORM

Transformation is ongoing. It can be toward or away from God's Will and purpose. Moving away from God's Will and purpose is transformation that occurs from making free-will choices that are Human Identity-driven. Moving toward God's Will and purpose is, from free-will choices that are Spirit Identity-driven and in some ways is moving forward and backward at the same time. Moving forward to increase God's Love through us. Moving backward to restore God's original human design of us.

CHAPTER 1: BE

THERE'S A WORD
THAT LOVED ME FROM THE START
A SOUND I HEARD
THAT TELLS ME OF MY WORTH
AND NOW I'VE LEARNED
WHO I REALLY AM
AND WHERE I STAND
AS A CHILD OF GOD

~Scott DeClaire Jr
'War of Thoughts'

(@ scottdeclairejr.com)

Day 1

Therefore if anyone is in Christ, this person is a new creation; the old things passed away; behold, new things have come.

2 Corinthians 5:17

As my Identity to BE, Holy Spirit is revealing to me…

Day 2

Or do you not know that your body is a temple of the Holy Spirit within you, whom you have from God, and that you are not your own? For you have been bought for a price: therefore glorify God in your body.

1 Corinthians 6:19-20

As my Identity to BE, Holy Spirit is revealing to me…

Day 3

See how great a love the Father has given us, that we would be called children of God; and in fact we are…Beloved, now we are children of God…We know that when He appears, we will be like Him.

1 John 3:1-2

As my Identity to BE, Holy Spirit is revealing to me…

Day 4

...as the truth is in Jesus, to put off your old self, which belongs to your former manner of life and is corrupt through deceitful desires, and to be renewed in the spirit of your minds, and to put on the new self, created after the likeness of God in true righteousness and holiness.

Ephesians 4:22-24

As my Identity to BE, Holy Spirit is revealing to me...

Day 5

Act as free people, and do not use your freedom as a covering for evil, but use it as bond-servants of God.

1 Peter 2:16

As my Identity to BE, Holy Spirit is revealing to me...

Day 6

And coming to Him as to a living stone which has been rejected by people, but is choice and precious in the sight of God, you also, as living stones, are being built up as a spiritual house for a holy priesthood, to offer spiritual sacrifices that are acceptable to God through Jesus Christ.

1 Peter 2:4-5

As my Identity to BE, Holy Spirit is revealing to me…

Day 7

But you are a chosen people, a royal priesthood, a holy nation, a people for Gods own possession, so that you may proclaim the excellencies of Him who has called you out of darkness into His marvelous light;

1 Peter 2:9

As my Identity to BE, Holy Spirit is revealing to me…

Day 8

For the Lord will not abandon His people on account of His great name, because the Lord has been pleased to make you a people for Himself.

1 Samuel 12:22

As my Identity to BE, Holy Spirit is revealing to me…

Day 9

But the Lord said to Samuel, "Do not look at his appearance or at the height of his stature, because I have rejected him; for God does not see as man sees, since man looks at the outward appearance, but the Lord looks at the heart."

1 Samuel 16:7

As my Identity to BE, Holy Spirit is revealing to me…

Day 10

But the one who is spiritual discerns all things, yet he himself is discerned by no one.

1 Corinthians 2:15

As my Identity to BE, Holy Spirit is revealing to me...

Day 11

And when you were dead in your wrongdoings and the uncircumcision of your flesh, He made you alive together with Him, having forgiven us all our wrongdoings,

Colossians 2:13

As my Identity to BE, Holy Spirit is revealing to me…

Day 12

If then you have been raised with Christ, seek the things that are above, where Christ is, seated at the right hand of God. Set your minds on things that are above, not on things that are on earth.

Colossians 3:1-2

As my Identity to BE, Holy Spirit is revealing to me...

Day 13

Paul, an apostle of Christ Jesus by the will of God, to the saints who are at Ephesus and are faithful in Christ Jesus:

Ephesians 1:1

As my Identity to BE, Holy Spirit is revealing to me...

Day 14

just as He chose us in Him before the foundation of the world, that we would be holy and blameless before Him. In love

Ephesians 1:4

As my Identity to BE, Holy Spirit is revealing to me...

Day 15

He predestined us to adoption as sons and daughters through Jesus Christ to Himself, according to the good pleasure of His will,

Ephesians 1:5

As my Identity to BE, Holy Spirit is revealing to me…

Day 16

For we are His workmanship, created in Christ Jesus for good works, which God prepared beforehand so that we would walk in them.

Ephesians 2:10

As my Identity to BE, Holy Spirit is revealing to me…

Day 17

So then you are no longer strangers and foreigners, but you are fellow citizens with the saints, and are of God's household,

Ephesians 2:19

As my Identity to BE, Holy Spirit is revealing to me...

Day 18

for you were once darkness, but now you are light in the Lord; walk as children of light

Ephesians 5:8

As my Identity to BE, Holy Spirit is revealing to me...

Day 19

For you are all sons and daughters of God through faith in Christ Jesus.

Galatians 3:26

As my Identity to BE, Holy Spirit is revealing to me…

Day 20

There is neither Jew nor Greek, there is neither slave nor free, there is neither male nor female; for you are all one in Christ Jesus.

Galatians 3:28

As my Identity to BE, Holy Spirit is revealing to me…

Day 21

And if you belong to Christ, then you are Abraham's descendants, heirs according to promise.

Galatians 3:29

As my Identity to BE, Holy Spirit is revealing to me…

Day 22

So God created man in His own image, in the image of God He created him; male and female He created them.

Genesis 1:27

As my Identity to BE, Holy Spirit is revealing to me…

Day 23

Then the Lord God formed the man of dust from the ground, and breathed into his nostrils the breath of life; and the man became a living person.

Genesis 2:7

As my Identity to BE, Holy Spirit is revealing to me...

Day 24

But now, this is what the Lord says, He who is your Creator, Jacob, and He who formed you, Israel: "Do not fear, for I have redeemed you; I have called you by name; you are Mine!

Isaiah 43:1

As my Identity to BE, Holy Spirit is revealing to me…

Day 25

Behold, I have inscribed you on the palms of My hands; Your walls are continually before Me.

Isaiah 49:16

As my Identity to BE, Holy Spirit is revealing to me…

Day 26

But now, Lord, You are our Father; we are the clay, and You our potter, and all of us are the work of Your hand.

Isaiah 64:8

As my Identity to BE, Holy Spirit is revealing to me…

Day 27

Before I formed you in the womb I knew you, and before you were born I consecrated you; I have appointed you as a prophet to the nations.

Jeremiah 1:5

As my Identity to BE, Holy Spirit is revealing to me…

Day 28

But as many as received Him, to them He gave the right to become children of God, to those who believe in His name,

John 1:12

As my Identity to BE, Holy Spirit is revealing to me…

Day 29

No longer do I call you slaves, for the slave does not know what his master is doing; but I have called you friends, because all things that I have heard from My Father I have made known to you.

John 15:15

As my Identity to BE, Holy Spirit is revealing to me...

Day 30

I am the vine, you are the branches; the one who remains in Me, and I in him bears much fruit, for apart from Me you can do nothing.

John 15:5

As my Identity to BE, Holy Spirit is revealing to me…

Day 31

So do not fear; you are more valuable than a great number of sparrows.

Matthew 10:31

As my Identity to BE, Holy Spirit is revealing to me…

Day 32

"You are the light of the world. A city set on a hill cannot be hidden;

Matthew 5:14

As my Identity to BE, Holy Spirit is revealing to me…

Day 33

Therefore you shall be perfect, as your heavenly Father is perfect.

Matthew 5:48

As my Identity to BE, Holy Spirit is revealing to me…

Day 34

Look at the birds of the sky, that they do not sow, nor reap, nor gather crops into barns, and yet your heavenly Father feeds them. Are you not much more important than they?

Matthew 6:26

As my Identity to BE, Holy Spirit is revealing to me...

Day 35

For our citizenship is in heaven, from which we also eagerly wait for a Savior, the Lord Jesus Christ;

Philippians 3:20

As my Identity to BE, Holy Spirit is revealing to me...

Day 36

Rejoice in the Lord always; again I will say, rejoice! Let your gentle spirit be known to all people. The Lord is near.

Philippians 4:4-5

As my Identity to BE, Holy Spirit is revealing to me...

Day 37

Know that the Lord Himself is God; it is He who has made us, and not we ourselves; we are His people and the sheep of His pasture.

Psalms 100:3

As my Identity to BE, Holy Spirit is revealing to me...

Day 38

I will give thanks to You, because I am awesomely and wonderfully made; wonderful are Your works, and my soul knows it very well.

Psalms 139:14

As my Identity to BE, Holy Spirit is revealing to me…

Day 39

So you too, consider yourselves to be dead to sin, but alive to God in Christ Jesus.

Romans 6:11

As my Identity to BE, Holy Spirit is revealing to me…

Day 40

knowing this, that our old self was crucified with Him, in order that our body of sin might be done away with, so that we would no longer be slaves to sin;

Romans 6:6

As my Identity to BE, Holy Spirit is revealing to me…

Day 41

Therefore there is now no condemnation at all for those who are in Christ Jesus.

Romans 8:1

As my Identity to BE, Holy Spirit is revealing to me…

Day 42

For you have not received a spirit of slavery leading to fear again, but you have received a spirit of adoption as sons and daughters by which we cry out, "Abba! Father!"

Romans 8:15

As my Identity to BE, Holy Spirit is revealing to me...

Day 43

and if children, heirs also, heirs of God and fellow heirs with Christ, if indeed we suffer with Him so that we may also be glorified with Him.

Romans 8:17

As my Identity to BE, Holy Spirit is revealing to me...

CHAPTER 2: HAVE

I HAVE YOUR THOUGHTS
I HEAR YOUR VOICE
YOUR LOVE LEADS ME
YOUR WAYS ARE MY CHOICE

I AM FREE
IN MY IDENTITY
TO TRULY BE
HOW YOU CREATED ME

~ 'We Are One'
by Jason Lohrke and Paula Lohrke-Moyer

(@ jesuscentricmind.com)

Day 44

But it is due to Him that you are in Christ Jesus, who became to us wisdom from God, and righteousness and sanctification, and redemption,

1 Corinthians 1:30

As my Identity to HAVE, Holy Spirit is revealing to me…

Day 45

Now you are Christ's body, and individually parts of it.

1 Corinthians 12:27

As my Identity to HAVE, Holy Spirit is revealing to me…

Day 46

but thanks be to God, who gives us the victory through our Lord Jesus Christ.

1 Corinthians 15:57

As my Identity to HAVE, Holy Spirit is revealing to me…

Day 47

For who has known the mind of the Lord, that he will instruct Him? But we have the mind of Christ.

1 Corinthians 2:16

As my Identity to HAVE, Holy Spirit is revealing to me...

Day 48

I am writing to you, little children, because your sins have been forgiven you on account of His name.

1 John 2:12

As my Identity to HAVE, Holy Spirit is revealing to me…

Day 49

And as for you, the anointing which you received from Him remains in you, and you have no need for anyone to teach you; but as His anointing teaches you about all things, and is true and is not a lie, and just as it has taught you, you remain in Him.

1 John 2:27

As my Identity to HAVE, Holy Spirit is revealing to me…

Day 50

Now He who establishes us with you in Christ and anointed us is God, who also sealed us and gave us the Spirit in our hearts as a pledge.

2 Corinthians 1:21-22

As my Identity to HAVE, Holy Spirit is revealing to me…

Day 51

Therefore, having such a hope, we use great boldness in our speech,

2 Corinthians 3:12

As my Identity to HAVE, Holy Spirit is revealing to me…

Day 52

Through these He has given us His very great and precious promises, so that through them you may participate in the divine nature, having escaped the corruption in the world caused by evil desires.

2 Peter 1:4

As my Identity to HAVE, Holy Spirit is revealing to me...

Day 53

For God has not given us a spirit of fear, but of power and of love and of a sound mind.

2 Timothy 1:7

As my Identity to HAVE, Holy Spirit is revealing to me...

Day 54

to whom God willed to make known what the wealth of the glory of this mystery among the Gentiles is, the mystery that is Christ in you, the hope of glory.

Colossians 1:27

As my Identity to HAVE, Holy Spirit is revealing to me…

Day 55

and in Him you have been made complete, and He is the head over every ruler and authority;

Colossians 2:10

As my Identity to HAVE, Holy Spirit is revealing to me…

Day 56

Therefore, as you have received Christ Jesus the Lord, so walk in Him, having been firmly rooted and now being built up in Him and established in your faith, just as you were instructed, and overflowing with gratitude.

Colossians 2:6-7

As my Identity to HAVE, Holy Spirit is revealing to me…

Day 57

In Him we also have obtained an inheritance, having been predestined according to the purpose of Him who works all things in accordance with the plan of His will,

Ephesians 1:11

As my Identity to HAVE, Holy Spirit is revealing to me…

Day 58

In Him, you also, after listening to the message of truth, the gospel of your salvation—having also believed, you were sealed in Him with the Holy Spirit of the promise,

Ephesians 1:13

As my Identity to HAVE, Holy Spirit is revealing to me…

Day 59

Blessed be the God and Father of our Lord Jesus Christ, who has blessed us with every spiritual blessing in the heavenly places in Christ,

Ephesians 1:3

As my Identity to HAVE, Holy Spirit is revealing to me…

Day 60

In Him we have redemption through His blood, the forgiveness of our wrongdoings, according to the riches of His grace

Ephesians 1:7

As my Identity to HAVE, Holy Spirit is revealing to me…

Day 61

But now in Christ Jesus you who previously were far away have been brought near by the blood of Christ.

Ephesians 2:13

As my Identity to HAVE, Holy Spirit is revealing to me…

Day 62

and raised us up with Him, and seated us with Him in the heavenly places in Christ Jesus,

Ephesians 2:6

As my Identity to HAVE, Holy Spirit is revealing to me…

Day 63

For by grace you have been saved through faith; and this is not of yourselves, it is the gift of God;

Ephesians 2:8

As my Identity to HAVE, Holy Spirit is revealing to me…

Day 64

in whom we have boldness and confident access through faith in Him.

Ephesians 3:12

As my Identity to HAVE, Holy Spirit is revealing to me…

Day 65

I have been crucified with Christ; and it is no longer I who live, but Christ lives in me; and the life which I now live in the flesh I live by faith in the Son of God, who loved me and gave Himself up for me.

Galatians 2:20

As my Identity to HAVE, Holy Spirit is revealing to me…

Day 66

For all of you who were baptized into Christ have clothed yourselves with Christ.

Galatians 3:27

As my Identity to HAVE, Holy Spirit is revealing to me...

Day 67

But He was pierced for our offenses, he was crushed for our wrongdoings; the punishment for our well-being was laid upon Him, and by His wounds we are healed.

Isaiah 53:5

As my Identity to HAVE, Holy Spirit is revealing to me…

Day 68

In righteousness you will be established; you will be far from oppression, for you will not fear; and from terror, for it will not come near you.

Isaiah 54:14

As my Identity to HAVE, Holy Spirit is revealing to me…

Day 69

For I know the plans I have for you, declares the Lord, plans to prosper you and not to harm you, plans to give you hope and a future.

Jeremiah 29:11

As my Identity to HAVE, Holy Spirit is revealing to me…

Day 70

Peace I leave you, My peace I give you; not as the world gives, do I give to you. Do not let your hearts be troubled, nor fearful.

John 14:27

As my Identity to HAVE, Holy Spirit is revealing to me...

Day 71

These things I have spoken to you so that My joy may be in you, and that your joy may be made full.

John 15:11

As my Identity to HAVE, Holy Spirit is revealing to me...

Day 72

Sanctify them in the truth; Your word is truth.

John 17:17

As my Identity to HAVE, Holy Spirit is revealing to me…

Day 73

"For God so loved the world, that He gave His only Son, so that everyone who believes in Him will not perish, but have eternal life.

John 3:16

As my Identity to HAVE, Holy Spirit is revealing to me...

Day 74

And my God will supply all your needs according to His riches in glory in Christ Jesus.

Philippians 4:19

As my Identity to HAVE, Holy Spirit is revealing to me…

Day 75

The God who encircles me with strength, and makes my way blameless?

Psalms 18:32

As my Identity to HAVE, Holy Spirit is revealing to me…

Day 76

To the one who overcomes, I will give some of the hidden manna, and I will give him a white stone, and a new name written on the stone which no one knows except the one who receives it.'

Revelations 2:17b

As my Identity to HAVE, Holy Spirit is revealing to me...

Day 77

Therefore, having been justified by faith, we have peace with God through our Lord Jesus Christ,

Romans 5:1

As my Identity to HAVE, Holy Spirit is revealing to me…

Day 78

For if by the offense of the one, death reigned through the one, much more will those who receive the abundance of grace and of the gift of righteousness reign in life through the One, Jesus Christ.

Romans 5:17

As my Identity to HAVE, Holy Spirit is revealing to me…

Day 79

And we know that God causes all things to work together for good to those who love God, to those who are called according to His purpose.

Romans 8:28

As my Identity to HAVE, Holy Spirit is revealing to me…

Day 80

The Lord your God is in your midst, a victorious warrior. He will rejoice over you with joy, He will be quiet in His love, He will rejoice over you with shouts of joy.

Zephaniah 3:17

As my Identity to HAVE, Holy Spirit is revealing to me…

CHAPTER 3:
DO

ABOVE ANYTHING
WE CAN DO FOR GOD,
OUR TRUST IN HIM
IS WHAT HE GENUINELY
DESIRES MOST.

~ 'Burn Your Ships'
Kelly Lohrke

(@ kellylohrke.com)

Day 81

Now the one who plants and the one who waters are one; but each will receive his own reward according to his own labor. For we are God's fellow workers; you are God's field, God's building.

1 Corinthians 3:8-9

In my Identity to DO, Holy Spirit is revealing to me...

Day 82

But the one who joins himself to the Lord is one spirit with Him.

1 Corinthians 6:17

In my Identity to DO, Holy Spirit is revealing to me…

Day 83

But sanctify Christ as Lord in your hearts, always being ready to make a defense to everyone who asks you to give an account for the hope that is in you, but with gentleness and respect;

1 Peter 3:15

In my Identity to DO, Holy Spirit is revealing to me…

Day 84

for we walk by faith, not by sight

2 Corinthians 5:7

In my Identity to DO, Holy Spirit is revealing to me…

Day 85

...make every effort to add to your faith goodness; and to goodness, knowledge; and to knowledge, self-control; and to self-control, perseverance; and to perseverance, godliness; and to godliness, mutual affection; and to mutual affection, love.

2 Peter 1:5:7

In my Identity to DO, Holy Spirit is revealing to me...

Day 86

be filled with the knowledge of His will in all spiritual wisdom and understanding, so that you will walk in a manner worthy of the Lord, to please Him in all respects, bearing fruit in every good work and increasing in the knowledge of God; strengthened with all power, according to His glorious might, for the attaining of all perseverance and patience; joyously giving thanks to the Father, who has qualified us to share in the inheritance of the saints in light.

Colossians 1:9b-12

In my Identity to DO, Holy Spirit is revealing to me…

____

____

____

____

____

____

____

Day 87

If you have died with Christ to the elementary principles of the world, why, as if you were living in the world, do you submit yourself to decrees

Colossians 2:20

In my Identity to DO, Holy Spirit is revealing to me…

Day 88

So, as those who have been chosen of God, holy and beloved, put on a heart of compassion, kindness, humility, gentleness, and patience;

Colossians 3:12

In my Identity to DO, Holy Spirit is revealing to me...

Day 89

For you have died, and your life is hidden with Christ and God. When Christ, who is our life, is revealed, then you also will be revealed with Him in glory.

Colossians 3:3-4

In my Identity to DO, Holy Spirit is revealing to me...

Day 90

And the Lord will make you the head and not the tail, and you will only be above, and not be underneath, if you listen to the commandments of the Lord your God which I am commanding you today, to follow them carefully,

Deuteronomy 28:13

In my Identity to DO, Holy Spirit is revealing to me…

Day 91

and to put on the new self, which in the likeness of God has been created in righteousness and holiness of the truth.

Ephesians 4:24

In my Identity to DO, Holy Spirit is revealing to me…

Day 92

For if you keep silent at this time, liberation and rescue will arise for the Jews from another place, and you and your father's house will perish. And who knows whether you have not attained royalty for such a time as this?"

Esther 4:14

In my Identity to DO, Holy Spirit is revealing to me...

Day 93

Bear one another's burdens, and thereby fulfill the law of Christ.

Galatians 6:2

In my Identity to DO, Holy Spirit is revealing to me…

Day 94

Your ears will hear a word behind you, saying, "This is the way, walk in it," whenever you turn to the right or to the left.

Isaiah 30:21

In my Identity to DO, Holy Spirit is revealing to me...

Day 95

Can the Ethiopian change his skin, or the leopard his spots? Then you as well can do good who are accustomed to doing evil.

Jeremiah 13:23

In my Identity to DO, Holy Spirit is revealing to me…

Day 96

"Set up roadmarks for yourself, place guideposts for yourself; direct your [a]mind to the highway, the way by which you went. Return, O virgin of Israel, return to these your cities.

Jeremiah 31:21

In my Identity to DO, Holy Spirit is revealing to me...

Day 97

Just as the Father has loved Me, I also have loved you; remain in My love.

John 15:9

In my Identity to DO, Holy Spirit is revealing to me...

Day 98

You did not choose Me but I chose you, and appointed you that you would go and bear fruit, and that your fruit would remain, so that whatever you ask of the Father in My name He may give to you.

John 15:16

In my Identity to DO, Holy Spirit is revealing to me...

Day 99

Have I not commanded you? Be strong and courageous! Do not be terrified nor dismayed, for the Lord your God is with you wherever you go."

Joshua 1:9

In my Identity to DO, Holy Spirit is revealing to me…

Day 100

Be merciful, just as your Father is merciful. "Do not judge, and you will not be judged; and do not condemn, and you will not be condemned; pardon, and you will be pardoned. Give, and it will be given to you. …For by your standard of measure it will be measured to you in return."

Luke 6:36-38

In my Identity to DO, Holy Spirit is revealing to me…

Day 101

…"If anyone wants to come after Me, he must deny himself, take up his cross daily, and follow Me. For whoever wants to save his life will lose it, but whoever loses his life for My sake, this is the one who will save it.

Matthew 16:24-25

In my Identity to DO, Holy Spirit is revealing to me…

Day 102

And the peace of God, which surpasses all comprehension, will guard your hearts and minds in Christ Jesus.

Philippians 4:7

In my Identity to DO, Holy Spirit is revealing to me...

Day 103

Therefore, accept one another, just as Christ also accepted us, for the glory of God.

Romans 15:7

In my Identity to DO, Holy Spirit is revealing to me…

Day 104

But in all these things we overwhelmingly conquer through Him who loved us.

Romans 8:37

In my Identity to DO, Holy Spirit is revealing to me…

PART 2: RENEW - REFORM

Renewing is restoration of God's original design for humans.

Humanity's connection with God fluctuates, like a radio frequency slightly or completely out of tune versus clearly in tune.

God is always broadcasting with secure and perfect purity. It is your turning of the dial to get on an unobstructed frequency with God that determines the clarity of the connection.

CHAPTER 4:
AS JESUS MODELED

**THERE IS A PLAN…
JESUS CAME TO
TAKE US OUT OF ADAM
IN AN EVER-INCREASING MANNER
SO WE CAN BECOME
MORE LIKE CHRIST.**

**~ Paster Don Sciortino
Net-Works Church Laguna Beach**

(@ lagunabeachnet-works.org)

Day 105

But if we walk in the Light as He Himself is in the Light, we have fellowship with one another, and the blood of Jesus His Son cleanses us from all sin.

1 John 1:7

In mind Renewing as Jesus Modeled, Holy Spirit reveals…

Day 106

Forasmuch then as Christ suffered for us in the flesh, arm yourselves also with the same mind; for he who has suffered in the flesh has ceased from sin;

1 Peter 4:1

In mind Renewing as Jesus Modeled, Holy Spirit reveals…

Day 107

If then you have been raised with Christ, seek the things that are above, where Christ is, seated at the right hand of God. Set your minds on things that are above, not on things that are on earth.

Colossians 3:1-2

In mind Renewing as Jesus Modeled, Holy Spirit reveals…

Day 108

For to this you were called, because Christ also suffered for us, leaving us an example, that you should follow His steps: "Who committed no sin, nor was deceit found in His mouth"; who, when He was reviled, did not revile in return; when He suffered, He did not threaten, but committed Himself to Him who judges righteously;

1 Peter 2:21-23

In mind Renewing as Jesus Modeled, Holy Spirit reveals…

____

____

____

____

____

____

____

____

____

Day 109

because it is written: "You shall be holy, for I am holy."

1 Peter 1:16

In mind Renewing as Jesus Modeled, Holy Spirit reveals…

Day 110

And He will delight in the fear of the Lord, and He will not judge by what His eyes see, nor make decisions by what His ears hear; But with righteousness He will judge the poor, and decide with fairness for the humble of the earth;

Isaiah 11:3-4

In mind Renewing as Jesus Modeled, Holy Spirit reveals...

Day 111

Peace I leave with you; my peace I give you. I do not give to you as the world gives. Do not let your hearts be troubled and do not be afraid.

John 14:27

In mind Renewing as Jesus Modeled, Holy Spirit reveals…

Day 112

...all the things that are written about Me in the Law of Moses and the Prophets and the Psalms must be fulfilled. Then He opened their minds to understand the Scriptures

Luke 24:44-45

In mind Renewing as Jesus Modeled, Holy Spirit reveals...

Day 113

...Truly I tell you, if you have faith and do not doubt, not only can you do what was done to the fig tree, but also you can say to this mountain, Go, throw yourself into the sea, and it will be done. If you believe, you will receive whatever you ask for in prayer.

Matthew 21:20-22

In mind Renewing as Jesus Modeled, Holy Spirit reveals...

Day 114

Teacher, which is the great commandment in the Law? And He said to him, You shall love the Lord your God with all your heart, and with all your soul, and with all your mind.

Matthew 22:36-37

In mind Renewing as Jesus Modeled, Holy Spirit reveals…

Day 115

Have this mind among yourselves, which is yours in Christ Jesus, who, though he was in the form of God, did not count equality with God a thing to be grasped, but emptied himself, by taking the form of a servant, being born in the likeness of men.

Philippians 2:5-7

In mind Renewing as Jesus Modeled, Holy Spirit reveals…

Day 116

He saved us, not because of righteous things we had done, but because of his mercy. He saved us through the washing of rebirth and renewal by the Holy Spirit,

Titus 3:5

In mind Renewing as Jesus Modeled, Holy Spirit reveals…

CHAPTER 5: SUPERNATURAL

THE MOMENT WE BELIEVE, GOD SENDS HIS SPIRIT IN US AND WE LIVE A NEW LIFE.

~ Pastor Jay Grant
Net-Works Church Laguna Beach

(@ lagunabeachnet-works.org)

Day 117

For if I pray in a tongue, my spirit prays but my mind is unfruitful. What am I to do? I will pray with my spirit, but I will pray with my mind also; I will sing praise with my spirit, but I will sing with my mind also.

1 Corinthians 14:14-15

In Supernatural mind Renewing, Holy Spirit reveals…

Day 118

But if an unbeliever or an inquirer comes in while everyone is prophesying, they are convicted of sin and are brought under judgment by all, as the secrets of their hearts are laid bare. So they will fall down and worship God, exclaiming, God is really among you!

1 Corinthians 14:24-25

In Supernatural mind Renewing, Holy Spirit reveals…

Day 119

Watch, stand fast in the faith, be brave, be strong. Let all that you do be done with love.

1 Corinthians 16:13-4

In Supernatural mind Renewing, Holy Spirit reveals…

Day 120

For who among people knows the thoughts of a person except the spirit of the person that is in him? So also the thoughts of God no one knows, except the Spirit of God. Now we have not received the spirit of the world, but the Spirit who is from God, so that we may know the things freely given to us by God.

1 Corinthians 2:11-12

In Supernatural mind Renewing, Holy Spirit reveals...

Day 121

But the one who is spiritual discerns all things, yet he himself is discerned by no one. For who has known the mind of the Lord, that he will instruct Him? But we have the mind of Christ.

1 Corinthians 2:15-16

In Supernatural mind Renewing, Holy Spirit reveals…

Day 122

Therefore, with minds that are alert and fully sober, set your hope on the grace to be brought to you when Jesus Christ is revealed at his coming.

1 Peter 1:13

In Supernatural mind Renewing, Holy Spirit reveals...

Day 123

Finally, brothers, rejoice. Be perfected, be comforted, be of the same mind, live in peace, and the God of love and peace will be with you.

2 Corinthians 13:11

In Supernatural mind Renewing, Holy Spirit reveals…

Day 124

For God has not given us a spirit of fear, but of power and of love and of a sound mind.

2 Timothy 1:7

In Supernatural mind Renewing, Holy Spirit reveals…

Day 125

All Scripture is breathed out by God and profitable for teaching, for reproof, for correction, and for training in righteousness.

2 Timothy 3:16

In Supernatural mind Renewing, Holy Spirit reveals…

Day 126

Thanks be to God through Jesus Christ our Lord! So then, on the one hand I myself with my mind am serving the law of God, but on the other, with my flesh the law of sin.

Romans 7:25

In Supernatural mind Renewing, Holy Spirit reveals…

Day 127

Do not lie to each other, since you have taken off your old self with its practices and have put on the new self, which is being renewed in knowledge in the image of its Creator.

Colossians 3:9-10

In Supernatural mind Renewing, Holy Spirit reveals…

Day 128

But as for me, this secret has not been revealed to me for any wisdom residing in me more than in any other living person, but for the purpose of making the interpretation known to the king, and that you may understand the thoughts of your mind.

Daniel 2:30

In Supernatural mind Renewing, Holy Spirit reveals...

Day 129

Hear, Israel! The Lord is our God, the Lord is one! And you shall love the Lord your God with all your heart and with all your soul and with all your strength. These words, which I am commanding you today, shall be on your heart.

Deuteronomy 6:4-6

In Supernatural mind Renewing, Holy Spirit reveals…

Day 130

Have I not commanded you? Be strong and courageous. Do not be frightened, and do not be dismayed, for the Lord your God is with you wherever you go.

Joshua 1:9

In Supernatural mind Renewing, Holy Spirit reveals…

Day 131

Moreover, I will give you a new heart and put a new spirit within you; and I will remove the heart of stone from your flesh and give you a heart of flesh. And I will put My Spirit within you and bring it about that you walk in My statutes, and are careful and follow My ordinances.

Ezekiel 36:26-27

In Supernatural mind Renewing, Holy Spirit reveals…

____

____

____

____

____

____

____

____

____

____

Day 132

The secret things belong to the LORD our God, but those things which are revealed belong to us and to our children forever, that we may do all the words of this law.

Deuteronomy 29:29

In Supernatural mind Renewing, Holy Spirit reveals…

Day 133

And without faith it is impossible to please God, because anyone who comes to Him must believe that He exists and that He rewards those who earnestly seek Him.

Hebrews 11:6

In Supernatural mind Renewing, Holy Spirit reveals…

Day 134

For the word of God is living and active, and sharper than any two-edged sword, even penetrating as far as the division of soul and spirit, of both joints and marrow, and able to judge the thoughts and intentions of the heart.

Hebrews 4:12

In Supernatural mind Renewing, Holy Spirit reveals…

Day 135

This is the covenant I will establish with the people of Israel after that time, declares the Lord. I will put my laws in their minds and write them on their hearts. I will be their God, and they will be my people.

Hebrews 8:10

In Supernatural mind Renewing, Holy Spirit reveals...

Day 136

My people are destroyed for lack of knowledge.

Hosea 4:6a

In Supernatural mind Renewing, Holy Spirit reveals…

Day 137

Come now, and let us reason together, says the Lord, though your sins are like scarlet, they shall be as white as snow; Though they are red like crimson, they shall be as wool.

Isaiah 1:18

In Supernatural mind Renewing, Holy Spirit reveals...

Day 138

Remember not the former things, nor consider the things of old. Behold, I am doing a new thing; now it springs forth, do you not perceive it? I will make a way in the wilderness and rivers in the desert.

Isaiah 43:18-19

In Supernatural mind Renewing, Holy Spirit reveals…

Day 139

If any of you lacks wisdom, let him ask God, who gives generously to all without reproach, and it will be given him. But let him ask in faith, with no doubting…For that person must not suppose that he will receive anything from the Lord; he is a double-minded man, unstable in all his ways.

James 1:5-8

In Supernatural mind Renewing, Holy Spirit reveals…

Day 140

I the LORD search the heart and test the mind, to give every man according to his ways, according to the fruit of his deeds.

Jeremiah 17:10

In Supernatural mind Renewing, Holy Spirit reveals…

Day 141

For I know the plans I have for you, declares the Lord, plans to prosper you and not to harm you, plans to give you hope and a future.

Jeremiah 29:11

In Supernatural mind Renewing, Holy Spirit reveals…

Day 142

Call to me and I will answer you, and will tell you great and hidden things that you have not known.

Jeremiah 33:3

In Supernatural mind Renewing, Holy Spirit reveals...

Day 143

Who has put wisdom in the inward parts or given understanding to the mind?

Job 38:36

In Supernatural mind Renewing, Holy Spirit reveals…

Day 144

I can do all things through Him who strengthens me.

Philippians 4:13

In Supernatural mind Renewing, Holy Spirit reveals...

Day 145

And the peace of God, which transcends all understanding, will guard your hearts and your minds in Christ Jesus.

Philippians 4:7

In Supernatural mind Renewing, Holy Spirit reveals...

Day 146

The mind of a person plans his way, but the Lord directs his steps.

Proverbs 16:9

In Supernatural mind Renewing, Holy Spirit reveals...

Day 147

The spirit of a person is the lamp of the Lord, searching all the innermost parts of his being.

Proverbs 20:27

In Supernatural mind Renewing, Holy Spirit reveals…

Day 148

Blows that hurt cleanse away evil, as do stripes the inner depths of the heart.

Proverbs 20:30

In Supernatural mind Renewing, Holy Spirit reveals…

Day 149

Every person's way is right in his own eyes, but the Lord examines the hearts.

Proverbs 21:2

In Supernatural mind Renewing, Holy Spirit reveals…

Day 150

Behold, You desire truth in the innermost being, and in secret You will make wisdom known to me.

Psalms 51:6

In Supernatural mind Renewing, Holy Spirit reveals…

Day 151

One who trusts in his own heart is a fool, but one who walks wisely will flee to safety.

Proverbs 28:26

In Supernatural mind Renewing, Holy Spirit reveals…

Day 152

May my meditation be pleasing to Him, as I rejoice in the Lord.

Proverbs 104:34

In Supernatural mind Renewing, Holy Spirit reveals…

Day 153

Let my cry come before You, Lord; Give me understanding according to Your word. Let my pleading come before You; Save me according to Your word. Let my lips pour out praise, For You teach me Your statutes.

Psalms 119:169-171

In Supernatural mind Renewing, Holy Spirit reveals…

Day 154

Lord, You have searched me and known me. You know when I sit down and when I get up; You understand my thought from far away.

Psalms 139:1-2

In Supernatural mind Renewing, Holy Spirit reveals...

Day 155

Search me, O God, and know my heart! Try me and know my thoughts! And see if there be any grievous way in me, and lead me in the way everlasting!

Psalms 139:23-24

In Supernatural mind Renewing, Holy Spirit reveals...

Day 156

I will bless the Lord who has advised me;
Indeed, my mind instructs me in the night.

Psalms 16:7

In Supernatural mind Renewing, Holy Spirit reveals…

Day 157

But who can discern their own errors? Forgive my hidden faults. Keep your servant also from willful sins; may they not rule over me. Then I will be blameless innocent of great transgression.

Psalms 19:12-13

In Supernatural mind Renewing, Holy Spirit reveals…

Day 158

Let the words of my mouth and the meditation of my heart be acceptable in your sight, O Lord, my rock and my redeemer.

Psalms 19:14

In Supernatural mind Renewing, Holy Spirit reveals...

Day 159

Prove me, O LORD, and try me; test my heart and my mind.

Psalms 26:2

In Supernatural mind Renewing, Holy Spirit reveals…

Day 160

Behold, You desire truth in the innermost being, and in secret You will make wisdom known to me.

Psalms 51:6

In Supernatural mind Renewing, Holy Spirit reveals…

Day 161

He who instructs the nations, shall He not correct, He who teaches man knowledge? The Lord knows the thoughts of man, that they are futile.

Psalms 94:10-11

In Supernatural mind Renewing, Holy Spirit reveals...

Day 162

And do not be conformed to this world, but be transformed by the renewing of your mind, so that you may prove what the will of God is, that which is good and acceptable and perfect.

Romans 12:2

In Supernatural mind Renewing, Holy Spirit reveals…

Day 163

Now may the God of patience and comfort grant you to be like-minded toward one another, according to Christ Jesus, that you may with one mind and one mouth glorify the God and Father of our Lord Jesus Christ.

Romans 15:5-6

In Supernatural mind Renewing, Holy Spirit reveals…

Day 164

For I joyfully agree with the law of God in the inner person, but I see a different law in the parts of my body waging war against the law of my mind, and making me a prisoner of the law of sin, the law which is in my body's parts.

Romans 7:22-23

In Supernatural mind Renewing, Holy Spirit reveals…

Day 165

And he who searches hearts knows what is the mind of the Spirit, because the Spirit intercedes for the saints according to the will of God.

Romans 8:27

In Supernatural mind Renewing, Holy Spirit reveals…

Day 166

And without faith it is impossible to please God, because anyone who comes to Him must believe that He exists and that He rewards those who earnestly seek Him.

Romans 8:7

In Supernatural mind Renewing, Holy Spirit reveals…

CHAPTER 6: MANAGE YOUR MIND

THE SPIRIT OF GOD COMES AND MAKES A HOME IN US. GOD MADE US TO BE INTIMATELY RELATED TO HIM.

~ Pastor Don Sciortino
Net-Works Church Laguna Beach

(@ lagunabeachnet-works.org)

Day 167

…serve Him with a perfect heart and with a willing mind; for the LORD searches all hearts, and understands all the imaginations of the thoughts.

1 Chronicles 28:9

In Renewing with Mind Management, Holy Spirit reveals…

Day 168

...you all speak the same thing and that there be no divisions among you, but that you be perfected together in the same mind and in the same judgment.

1 Corinthians 1:10

In Renewing with Mind Management, Holy Spirit reveals...

Day 169

Brothers and sisters, stop thinking like children. In regard to evil be infants, but in your thinking be adults.

1 Corinthians 14:20

In Renewing with Mind Management, Holy Spirit reveals…

Day 170

Do not deceive yourselves. If any of you think you are wise by the standards of this age, you should become fools so that you may become wise.

1 Corinthians 3:18

In Renewing with Mind Management, Holy Spirit reveals…

Day 171

But the end of all things is near. Therefore be of sound mind, self-controlled, and sober in prayer.

1 Peter 4:7

In Renewing with Mind Management, Holy Spirit reveals…

Day 172

We demolish arguments and every pretension that sets itself up against the knowledge of God, and we take captive every thought to make it obedient to Christ.

2 Corinthians 10:3-5

In Renewing with Mind Management, Holy Spirit reveals…

Day 173

For if we are beside ourselves, it is for God. Or if we are of sober mind, it is for you.

2 Corinthians 5:13

In Renewing with Mind Management, Holy Spirit reveals...

Day 174

…I am stirring up your sincere mind by way of a reminder, to remember the words spoken beforehand by the holy prophets and the commandment of the Lord and Savior spoken by your apostles.

2 Peter 3:1-2

In Renewing with Mind Management, Holy Spirit reveals…

Day 175

Now, brethren, concerning the coming of our Lord Jesus Christ and our gathering together to Him, we ask you, not to be soon shaken in mind or troubled, either by spirit or by word or by letter, as if from us, as though the day of Christ had come.

2 Thessalonians 2:1-2

In Renewing with Mind Management, Holy Spirit reveals…

Day 176

Now these were more noble than those in Thessalonica, in that they received the word with all readiness of the mind, examining the Scriptures daily to see whether these things were so.

Acts 17:11

In Renewing with Mind Management, Holy Spirit reveals...

Day 177

This I say therefore, and testify in the Lord, that you no longer walk as the rest of the Gentiles also walk, in the futility of their mind,

Ephesians 4:17

In Renewing with Mind Management, Holy Spirit reveals…

Day 178

In your anger do not sin: Do not let the sun go down while you are still angry, and do not give the devil a foothold.

Ephesians 4:26-27

In Renewing with Mind Management, Holy Spirit reveals…

Day 179

Do not let any unwholesome talk come out of your mouths, but only what is helpful for building others up according to their needs, that it may benefit those who listen.

Ephesians 4:29

In Renewing with Mind Management, Holy Spirit reveals…

Day 180

Get rid of all bitterness, rage and anger, brawling and slander, along with every form of malice. Be kind and compassionate to one another, forgiving each other, just as in Christ God forgave you.

Ephesians 4:31-32

In Renewing with Mind Management, Holy Spirit reveals…

Day 181

...Anyone of the house of Israel who sets up his idols in his heart, puts in front of his face the stumbling block of his wrongdoing, and then comes to the prophet, I the Lord will let Myself answer him in the matter in view of the multitude of his idols,

Ezekiel 14:4

In Renewing with Mind Management, Holy Spirit reveals...

Day 182

Keep your lives free from the love of money and be content with what you have, because God has said, Never will I leave you; never will I forsake you.

Hebrew 12:15

In Renewing with Mind Management, Holy Spirit reveals…

Day 183

Keep your lives free from the love of money and be content with what you have, because God has said, Never will I leave you; never will I forsake you.

Hebrew 13:5

In Renewing with Mind Management, Holy Spirit reveals…

Day 184

You will keep in perfect peace those whose minds are steadfast, because they trust in You.

Isaiah 26:3

In Renewing with Mind Management, Holy Spirit reveals...

Day 185

This Book of the Law shall not depart from your mouth, but you shall meditate on it day and night, so that you may be careful to do according to all that is written in it. For then you will make your way prosperous, and then you will have good success.

Josiah 1:8

In Renewing with Mind Management, Holy Spirit reveals...

Day 186

For it is from within, out of a person's heart, that evil thoughts come sexual immorality, theft, murder, adultery, greed, malice, deceit, lewdness, envy, slander, arrogance and folly.

Mark 7:21-22

In Renewing with Mind Management, Holy Spirit reveals…

Day 187

It is not what enters the mouth that defiles the person, but what comes out of the mouth, this defiles the person.

Matthew 15:11

In Renewing with Mind Management, Holy Spirit reveals...

Day 188

It is not what enters the mouth that defiles the person, but what comes out of the mouth, this defiles the person.

Matthew 6:25

In Renewing with Mind Management, Holy Spirit reveals…

Day 189

So if there is any encouragement in Christ, any comfort from love, any participation in the Spirit, any affection and sympathy, complete my joy by being of the same mind, having the same love, being in full accord and of one mind.

Philippians 2:1-2

In Renewing with Mind Management, Holy Spirit reveals...

Day 190

Do not be anxious about anything, but in everything by prayer and supplication with thanksgiving let your requests be made known to God.

Philippians 4:6

In Renewing with Mind Management, Holy Spirit reveals…

Day 191

Finally, brothers and sisters, whatever is true, whatever is honorable, whatever is right, whatever is pure, whatever is lovely, whatever is commendable, if there is any excellence and if anything worthy of praise, think about these things.

Philippians 4:8

In Renewing with Mind Management, Holy Spirit reveals…

Day 192

The heart of the righteous weighs its answers, but the mouth of the wicked gushes evil.

Proverbs 15:28

In Renewing with Mind Management, Holy Spirit reveals…

Day 193

A cheerful heart is good medicine, but a crushed spirit dries up the bones.

Proverbs 17:22

In Renewing with Mind Management, Holy Spirit reveals…

Day 194

The words of a gossiper are like dainty morsels, and they go down into the innermost parts of the body.

Proverbs 18:8

In Renewing with Mind Management, Holy Spirit reveals…

Day 195

Trust in the Lord with all your heart, and do not lean on your own understanding.

Proverbs 3:5

In Renewing with Mind Management, Holy Spirit reveals…

Day 196

Give careful thought to the paths for your feet and be steadfast in all your ways.

Proverbs 4:26

In Renewing with Mind Management, Holy Spirit reveals…

Day 197

My son, keep my words and store up my commands within you. Keep my commands and you will live; guard my teachings as the apple of your eye. Bind them on your fingers; write them on the tablet of your heart.

Proverbs 7:1-3

In Renewing with Mind Management, Holy Spirit reveals…

Day 198

I have treasured Your word in my heart, so that I may not sin against You.

Psalms 119:11

In Renewing with Mind Management, Holy Spirit reveals…

Day 199

Furthermore, just as they did not think it worthwhile to retain the knowledge of God, so God gave them over to a depraved mind, so that they do what ought not to be done.

Romans 1:28

In Renewing with Mind Management, Holy Spirit reveals…

Day 200

...Do not think of yourself more highly than you ought, but rather think of yourself with sober judgment, in accordance with the faith God has distributed to each of you.

Romans 12:3

In Renewing with Mind Management, Holy Spirit reveals...

Day 201

For to set the mind on the flesh is death, but to set the mind on the Spirit is life and peace.

Romans 8:6

In Renewing with Mind Management, Holy Spirit reveals...

PART 3: LOVE - UNIFORM

Love is the great unifier. It encompasses and blankets all of us.

God, as love, seeing us all equally deserving of acceptance, value, and validation.

Love is the action of God to us and then through us to others, knowingly and unknowingly.

You have free-will choice to intentionally participate.

CHAPTER 7: WHAT LOVE IS

THE LOVE OF GOD
IS SET UPON YOU
AND UPON ME
FOREVER AND EVER.

IT IS AN UNBREAKABLE LOVE.
IT IS AN UNCHANGING LOVE.
IT IS A LOVE
WITH NO CONDITIONS.
IT'S A LOVE
THAT IS IRREVOCABLE.
IT'S ALWAYS THERE FOR US.

~ Pastor Jay Grant
Net-Works Church Laguna Beach

(@ lagunabeachnet-works.org)

Day 202

Love is patient, love is kind…rejoices with the truth; it keeps every confidence, it believes all things, hopes all things, endures all things. Love never fails...

1 Corinthians 4-8a

What Love Is as God's Love, Holy Spirit reveals to me…

Day 203

See what kind of love the Father has given to us, that we should be called children of God; and so we are.

1 John 3:1a

What Love Is as God's Love, Holy Spirit reveals to me…

Day 204

And so we know and rely on the love God has for us. God is love. Whoever lives in love lives in God, and God in them. This is how love is made complete among us so that we will have confidence on the day of judgment: In this world we are like Jesus.

1 John 4:16b-17

What Love Is as God's Love, Holy Spirit reveals to me…

Day 205

Beloved, let's love one another; for love is from God, and everyone who loves has been born of God and knows God.

1 John 4:7

What Love Is as God's Love, Holy Spirit reveals to me…

Day 206

The one who does not love does not know God, because God is love.

1 John 4:8

What Love Is as God's Love, Holy Spirit reveals to me...

Day 207

Husbands, love your wives, just as Christ also loved the church and gave Himself up for her,

Ephesians 5:25

What Love Is as God's Love, Holy Spirit reveals to me…

Day 208

Nevertheless, as for you individually, each husband is to love his own wife the same as himself,

Ephesians 5:33

What Love Is as God's Love, Holy Spirit reveals to me...

Day 209

If you love Me, you will keep My commandments.

John 14:15

What Love Is as God's Love, Holy Spirit reveals to me…

Day 210

The one who has My commandments and keeps them is the one who loves Me; and the one who loves Me will be loved by My Father, and I will love him and will reveal Myself to him.

John 14:21

What Love Is as God's Love, Holy Spirit reveals to me...

Day 211

Jesus answered and said to him, "If anyone loves Me, he will follow My word; and My Father will love him, and We will come to him and make Our dwelling with him.

John 14:23

What Love Is as God's Love, Holy Spirit reveals to me…

Day 212

Greater love has no one than this, that a person lay down his life for his friends.

John 15:13

What Love Is as God's Love, Holy Spirit reveals to me...

Day 213

Love covers all rebellion.

Proverbs 10-12b

What Love Is as God's Love, Holy Spirit reveals to me…

Day 214

He loves righteousness and justice.

Psalms 33:5a

What Love Is as God's Love, Holy Spirit reveals to me...

CHAPTER 8:
GOD'S LOVE FOR US

THE SOULS OF
MEN AND WOMEN
ARE GOD'S
VALUABLE TREASURE.

~ Pastor Esther Lohrke
The Cure Church
Kansas City, KS

(@ thecure.church)

Day 215

Give thanks to the Lord, for He is good; His love endures forever.

1 Chronicles 16:34

As God's Love for Us, Holy Spirit reveals to me...

Day 216

We know love by this, that he laid down His life for us; and we ought to lay down our lives for the brothers and sisters.

1 John 3:16

As God's Love for Us, Holy Spirit reveals to me...

Day 217

In this is love, not that we have loved God but that he loved us

1 John 4:10a

As God's Love for Us, Holy Spirit reveals to me…

Day 218

No one has ever seen God; but if we love one another, God lives in us and His love is made complete in us.

1 John 4:12

As God's Love for Us, Holy Spirit reveals to me…

Day 219

May the Lord direct your hearts to the love of God and to the steadfastness of Christ.

2 Thessalonians 3:5

As God's Love for Us, Holy Spirit reveals to me...

Day 220

Now therefore that the Lord your God is God; He is the faithful God, keeping His covenant of love to a thousand generations of those who love Him and keep His commandments.

Deuteronomy 7:9

As God's Love for Us, Holy Spirit reveals to me…

Day 221

And he passed in front of Moses, proclaiming, "The Lord, the Lord, the compassionate and gracious God, slow to anger, abounding in love and faithfulness,

Exodus 34:6

As God's Love for Us, Holy Spirit reveals to me...

Day 222

For the Lord disciplines the one he loves, and chastises every son whom he receives.

Hebrews 12:6

As God's Love for Us, Holy Spirit reveals to me…

Day 223

Though the mountains be shaken and the hills be removed, yet my unfailing love for you will not be shaken nor my covenant of peace be removed, says the Lord, who has compassion on you.

Isaiah 54:10

As God's Love for Us, Holy Spirit reveals to me...

Day 224

I have loved you with an everlasting love; I have drawn you with unfailing kindness.

Jeremiah 31:3

As God's Love for Us, Holy Spirit reveals to me…

Day 225

Return to the LORD your God, for he is merciful and compassionate, patient and filled with unfailing love.

Joel 2:13b

As God's Love for Us, Holy Spirit reveals to me…

Day 226

Just as the Father has loved Me, I also have loved you; remain in My love. If you keep My commandments, you will remain in My love; just as I have kept My Father's commandments and remain in His love.

John 15:9-10

As God's Love for Us, Holy Spirit reveals to me…

Day 227

I in them and You in Me, that they may be perfected in unity, so that the world may know that You sent Me and You loved them, just as You love Me.

John 17:23

As God's Love for Us, Holy Spirit reveals to me…

Day 228

For God so loved the world, that He gave His only Son, so that everyone who believes in Him will not perish, but have eternal life.

John 3:16

As God's Love for Us, Holy Spirit reveals to me…

Day 229

But you, beloved, building yourselves up in your most holy faith and praying in the Holy Spirit, keep yourselves in the love of God,

Jude 1:20-21a

As God's Love for Us, Holy Spirit reveals to me...

Day 230

For the LORD is good; his steadfast love endures forever, and his faithfulness to all generations.

Psalms 100:5

As God's Love for Us, Holy Spirit reveals to me…

Day 231

For as high as the heavens are above the earth, So great is His lovingkindness toward those who fear Him. As far as the east is from the west, So far has he removed our transgressions from us.

Psalms 103:11-12

As God's Love for Us, Holy Spirit reveals to me…

Day 232

But the steadfast love of the Lord is from everlasting to everlasting on those who fear him, and his righteousness to children's children, to those who keep his covenant and remember to do his commandments.

Psalms 103:17-18

As God's Love for Us, Holy Spirit reveals to me…

Day 233

You are merciful, LORD! You are kind and patient and always loving.

Psalms 145:8

As God's Love for Us, Holy Spirit reveals to me…

Day 234

Lord, I love the refuge of your house, the site of the dwelling-place of your glory.

Psalms 26:8

As God's Love for Us, Holy Spirit reveals to me…

Day 235

You will protect them and those will rejoice in you who love your name.

Psalms 5:11b

As God's Love for Us, Holy Spirit reveals to me…

Day 236

Have mercy on me, God, according to your unfailing love;

Psalms 51:1a

As God's Love for Us, Holy Spirit reveals to me…

Day 237

Because thy lovingkindness is better than life, my lips shall praise thee.

Psalms 63:3

As God's Love for Us, Holy Spirit reveals to me…

Day 238

But you, Lord, are a compassionate and gracious God, slow to anger, abounding in love and faithfulness.

Psalms 86:15

As God's Love for Us, Holy Spirit reveals to me…

Day 239

To him who loves us and has freed us from our sins by his blood.

Revelations 1:5b

As God's Love for Us, Holy Spirit reveals to me…

Day 240

Hope does not put us to shame, because God's love has been poured into our hearts through the Holy Spirit who has been given to us.

Romans 5:5

As God's Love for Us, Holy Spirit reveals to me…

Day 241

But God proves His love for us in that while we were still sinners Christ died for us..

Romans 5:8

As God's Love for Us, Holy Spirit reveals to me…

Day 242

For I am convinced that neither death, nor life, not angels, nor principalities, nor things present, nor things to come, nor powers, nor height, nor depth, nor any other created thing will be able to separate us from the love of God that is in Christ Jesus our Lord.

Romans 8:37-39

As God's Love for Us, Holy Spirit reveals to me…

Day 243

But when the kindness of God our Savior and His love for mankind appeared, He saved us, not on the basis of deeds which we did in righteousness, but in accordance with His mercy, by the washing of regeneration and renewing by the Holy Spirit, whom He richly poured out upon us through Jesus Christ our Savior, so that being justified by His grace we would be made heirs according to the hope of eternal life.

Titus 3:4-7

As God's Love for Us, Holy Spirit reveals to me…

Day 244

The Lord your God is with you, the Mighty Warrior who saves. He will take great delight in you; in His love He will no longer rebuke you, but will rejoice over you with singing.

Zephaniah 3:17

As God's Love for Us, Holy Spirit reveals to me…

CHAPTER 9: GOD'S LOVE FROM US

BEING ABLE TO LOVE OUR ENEMIES,
AND THOSE WHO LIE AND
TALK BAD ABOUT US,
IS A SUPERNATURAL WORK
THAT GOD DOES THROUGH US.

YOU ARE NOT RESPONSIBLE
FOR CONJURING UP
THIS LOVE FROM SCRATCH.

IT'S A WORK OF THE HOLY SPIRIT.

~ 'Burn Your Ships'
Kelly Lohrke

(@ kellylohrke.com)

Day 245

We love, because He first loved us.

1 John 4:19

As God's Love going From Us, Holy Spirit reveals to me…

Day 246

Above all, love each other deeply, because love covers over a multitude of sins.

1 Peter 4:8

As God's Love going From Us, Holy Spirit reveals to me…

Day 247

Finally, brothers, rejoice. Aim for restoration, comfort one another, agree with one another, live in peace; and the God of love and peace will be with you.

2 Corinthians 13:11

As God's Love going From Us, Holy Spirit reveals to me…

Day 248

You shall love the Lord your God with all your heart and with all your soul and with all your might.

Deuteronomy 6:5

As God's Love going From Us, Holy Spirit reveals to me…

Day 249

Therefore, be imitators of God, as beloved children; and walk in love, just as Christ also loved you and gave Himself up for us, an offering and a sacrifice to God as a fragrant aroma.

Ephesians 5:1-2

As God's Love going From Us, Holy Spirit reveals to me…

Day 250

I am giving you a new commandment, that you love one another; just as I have loved you, that you also love one another. By this all people will know that you are My disciples: if you have love for one another.

John 13:34-35

As God's Love going From Us, Holy Spirit reveals to me…

Day 251

You have heard that it was said, 'You shall love your neighbor and hate your enemy.' But I say to you, love your enemies and pray for those who persecute you,

Matthew 5:43-44

As God's Love going From Us, Holy Spirit reveals to me…

Day 252

for I delight in your commands because I love them. I reach out for your commands, which I love, that I may meditate on your decrees.

Psalms 119:47-48

As God's Love going From Us, Holy Spirit reveals to me…

Day 253

Give thanks to the God of heaven, for his steadfast love endures forever.

Psalms 136:26

As God's Love going From Us, Holy Spirit reveals to me…

Day 254

I love you, Lord, my strength, Lord, my rock, my fortress, my deliverer, my God, my rock of refuge, my shield, my saving horn, my stronghold!

Psalms 18:1

As God's Love going From Us, Holy Spirit reveals to me...

Day 255

Love the Lord, all who are faithful to him. The Lord watches over the faithful.

Psalms 31:23a

As God's Love going From Us, Holy Spirit reveals to me…

Day 256

It is good to give thanks to the Lord, to sing praise to your name, Most High, to proclaim your love at daybreak, your faithfulness in the night,

Psalms 92:1-2

As God's Love going From Us, Holy Spirit reveals to me…

Day 257

Owe nothing to anyone except to love one another; for the one who loves his neighbor has fulfilled the law.

Romans 13:8

As God's Love going From Us, Holy Spirit reveals to me...

PART 4: MIND FINDS - PERFORM

These are revelatory learnings from Holy Spirit that we have received, integrated, and put into action in our lives.

We share them to encourage you as you have received and continue to receive revelatory learnings from Holy Spirit and live them out to experience the full measure as a human, standing in your God given power, as Jesus modeled, manifesting the Fruits of the Spirit.

CHAPTER 10: MEANING

WITH A LOVE LIKE YOURS,
THE PAST DOESN'T MATTER,
THOUGHTS SEEM TO SCATTER
OF HOW I USED TO BE.
WITH A LOVE LIKE YOURS,
I AM SECURE
IN ALL THAT LIFE BRINGS,
BECAUSE YOU FIRST LOVED ME.
YOU'RE MY FIRST LOVE,
I LONG FOR YOU.
YOU'RE MY FIRST LOVE,
OH JESUS, I BELONG WITH YOU.

~ 'Belong'
by Jason Lohrke and Paula Lohrke-Moyer

(@ jesuscentricmind.com)

Day 258

Shine God's light and love to your own soul by meditating and believing in what you're here to create.

#shinelove

In the Meaning of my identity, Holy Spirit reveals to me…

Day 259

Becoming consciously aware of your connection to the causal spirit realm happens by choice.
Keep...Growing...Forward.

#growforward

In the Meaning of my identity, Holy Spirit reveals to me…

Day 260

Struggle is a sign you're progressing and that you've outgrown something.

#proofofprogress

In the Meaning of my identity, Holy Spirit reveals to me...

Day 261

Keep your peace by refusing to blame others. Notice what thoughts and emotions are coming up as communication from Holy Spirit to you. Surrender to God-Love.

#triggeredlearning

In the Meaning of my identity, Holy Spirit reveals to me…

Day 262

Have gratitude for situations and people in your life that trigger you the most. It cracks open old wounds for healing and opportunities for you to extend love.

#crackopen

In the Meaning of my identity, Holy Spirit reveals to me…

Day 263

You're free to think whatever you want. And, thinking it's them...instead of you..is what's keeping you stuck. Now, go get unstuck.

#getunstuck

In the Meaning of my identity, Holy Spirit reveals to me…

Day 264

Your past influences your moment-of-now and your future...if you choose to let it.

#chooseyourinfluence

In the Meaning of my identity, Holy Spirit reveals to me…

Day 265

Let it define you OR Leave it behind you. Your Spirit Identity only sees only one choice.

#onechoice

In the Meaning of my identity, Holy Spirit reveals to me…

Day 266

Trying times are the perfect testing ground to strengthen your memory muscles about God's truth of your worth.

#truthofworth

In the Meaning of my identity, Holy Spirit reveals to me...

Day 267

This struggle you have is what you've been training for.

#trainingfor

In the Meaning of my identity, Holy Spirit reveals to me…

Day 268

Your mental fortitude lifts their mental fortitude.

#rolemodel

In the Meaning of my identity, Holy Spirit reveals to me…

Day 269

How you care for yourself demonstrates how you care for others.

#demonstratecare

In the Meaning of my identity, Holy Spirit reveals to me…

Day 270

Who you are BEing has outgrown what you are DOing.

#belikejesus

In the Meaning of my identity, Holy Spirit reveals to me…

Day 271

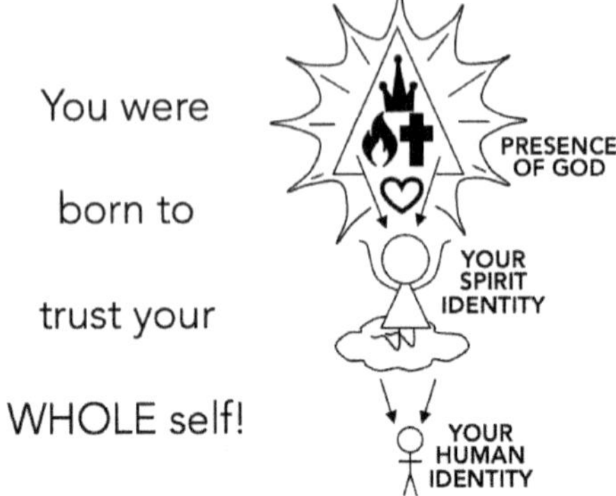

#wholeself

In the Meaning of my identity, Holy Spirit reveals to me…

Day 272

Good Wonder:
Wonder about God's creations.
Wonder if your awareness is big enough.
Wonder what your identity is.
Wonder how you can be like Jesus.
Wonder what Holy Spirit is teaching you.

#goodwonder

In the Meaning of my identity, Holy Spirit reveals to me...

___

___

___

___

___

___

___

___

___

___

___

Day 273

How you give to others determines how abundant your life will be.

#giveabundantly

In the Meaning of my identity, Holy Spirit reveals to me…

Day 274

Having clarity about your Spirit Identity is like having a forcefield around you. Everything unresourceful just bounces off.

#forcefield

In the Meaning of my identity, Holy Spirit reveals to me…

Day 275

People will be influenced by you even after you're gone. Be intentional about what influence you are having.

#intentionalinfluence

In the Meaning of my identity, Holy Spirit reveals to me…

Day 276

Your daily actions reveal your beliefs, values and identity. It all trickles down from who you are being.

#actions

In the Meaning of my identity, Holy Spirit reveals to me…

Day 277

Your ascension into the Presence of God for Eternity waits for you to remember who you are.

#wakeup

In the Meaning of my identity, Holy Spirit reveals to me…

Day 278

Success is living an earth-life legacy that ascends you and others to an eternal-life reality.

#legacytoascend

In the Meaning of my identity, Holy Spirit reveals to me...

Day 279

Being an Extension of God is like being a predator hunting to kill the belief that earth-life is all there is.

#killthebelief

In the Meaning of my identity, Holy Spirit reveals to me…

Day 280

Live the earth-life legacy that your Spirit Identity will warrior with you for.

#legacy

In the Meaning of my identity, Holy Spirit reveals to me...

Day 281

Choose to believe that unfamiliar actions in the physical realm are fun because it activates Holy Spirit's guidance through it which leads to supernatural spirit realm victory!

#winning

In the Meaning of my identity, Holy Spirit reveals to me…

Day 282

When you say YES to someone else so you can avoid discomfort, you're saying NO to all the wisdom you were equipped with.

#equipped

In the Meaning of my identity, Holy Spirit reveals to me…

Day 283

Staying aligned with who you know you are as an Extension of God's Love is a guaranteed way to shut out the lying voices.

#guaranteed

In the Meaning of my identity, Holy Spirit reveals to me...

Day 284

Your life will leave a mark on the hearts of others...that's the point.

#leaveamark

In the Meaning of my identity, Holy Spirit reveals to me...

Day 285

Your imprint will be high on those whose hearts you touch.

#touchhearts

In the Meaning of my identity, Holy Spirit reveals to me…

Day 286

The old version of you used to believe it was people or situations that were the problem. Now, you remember this earth-life is the chessboard and your King has already won!

#unstoppableking

In the Meaning of my identity, Holy Spirit reveals to me…

Day 287

Your Spirit Identity is resourceful and knows it's ability to work through difficult things.

#resourceful

In the Meaning of my identity, Holy Spirit reveals to me…

Day 288

The more you work to raise your awareness that you are more than your Human Identity, the easier it is to accept that some thoughts have run their course.

#youaremore

In the Meaning of my identity, Holy Spirit reveals to me…

Day 289

Only tolerate success because life is rigged in your favor.

#godsplan

In the Meaning of my identity, Holy Spirit reveals to me…

Day 290

A mirror is just a piece of glass. You are SOOOOOO much more than that. Like a LOT more.

#muchmore

In the Meaning of my identity, Holy Spirit reveals to me…

Day 291

People remember you because of how you have influenced them to remember who they are.

#influencehigher

In the Meaning of my identity, Holy Spirit reveals to me…

Day 292

Life DOES come with a manual...plus a mind, a body, a spirit, a creator, a model, a guide, and a purpose. Remember who you are, BEYOND this earth-life.

#biblemanualoflife

In the Meaning of my identity, Holy Spirit reveals to me...

Day 293

If they don't feel right about it, that's their responsibility. Yours is to make sure YOU do.

#feelright

In the Meaning of my identity, Holy Spirit reveals to me…

Day 294

Judging and Loving will always be at war with each other. Be Love. Let God handle the Judging stuff.

#belove

In the Meaning of my identity, Holy Spirit reveals to me…

Day 295

Your Spirit Identity is your greatest self-resource, and it knows all the answers you need are just a 'Holy Spirit ask' away.

#selfresource

In the Meaning of my identity, Holy Spirit reveals to me…

Day 296

The more you extend God's Love in the choices you make, the less it matters what others do.

#extendlove

In the Meaning of my identity, Holy Spirit reveals to me...

Day 297

Living to avoid the disapproval of others is sentencing yourself to repeat the things you've been working so hard to exit from.

#timetoexit

In the Meaning of my identity, Holy Spirit reveals to me…

Day 298

Standing up for yourself is gonna make some people uncomfortable. That's OK though, you're doing it right.

#keepstanding

In the Meaning of my identity, Holy Spirit reveals to me…

CHAPTER 11: EMOTIONS

I FEEL PEACE,
I FEEL LIGHT
I SEE MY STAINS
TURN PURE WHITE
I FEEL A BURDEN,
LIFT FROM ME
AS I RAISE MY HANDS
UP, AND I SING...
GLORY, GLORY, GLORY
TO THE KING

~ 'Glory to the King'
by Chris Lizotte

Day 299

Joy is a feeling you can have, only if YOU choose to have it.

#choosejoy

In the Emotions of my identity, Holy Spirit reveals to me…

Day 300

Surrender to God's Will and come face to face with any doubts. What you thought was fear is actually excitement because you are going ---> through ---> it.

#woohooo

In the Emotions of my identity, Holy Spirit reveals to me…

Day 301

You are choosing everything that you are emotionally experiencing. Trust the work God is doing through you, it's paving the path you have been training for.

#trustthework

In the Emotions of my identity, Holy Spirit reveals to me...

Day 302

When you accept that you are the manager of your emotional reality, you ascend your awareness of who God created you to be.

#manageemotionalreality

In the Emotions of my identity, Holy Spirit reveals to me…

Day 303

Continuing that reaction is a habit from an outdated version of you. Ask Holy Spirit what you need to learn, apply the learning to release the emotion so the emotion can serve its purpose and just go away now.

#itjustgoesaway

In the Emotions of my identity, Holy Spirit reveals to me...

Day 304

Your awareness of you being triggered because of past experiences is your responsibility. You are the time-travel engineer.

#timetravelengineer

In the Emotions of my identity, Holy Spirit reveals to me…

Day 305

Since you are the manager of your emotional reality, choose your experiences accordingly.

#chooseaccordingly

In the Emotions of my identity, Holy Spirit reveals to me...

Day 306

When I take responsibility for my experience, I am emotionally rockin' it!

#rockit

In the Emotions of my identity, Holy Spirit reveals to me…

Day 307

Giving or Receiving the silent treatment is a form of abuse. Instead, leverage the struggle to increase love.

#leveragestruggle

In the Emotions of my identity, Holy Spirit reveals to me…

Day 308

You are only responsible for YOUR emotional response.

#onlyyours

In the Emotions of my identity, Holy Spirit reveals to me…

Day 309

Few will be pleased with who you are being. Soooo ummm...

#thatsonthem

In the Emotions of my identity, Holy Spirit reveals to me...

Day 310

Your body can hear your thoughts...keep it positive.

#thinklove

In the Emotions of my identity, Holy Spirit reveals to me…

Day 311

Choose to leave behind the hurts from relationships in the past so you can love through the relationships you have now.

#lovethrough

In the Emotions of my identity, Holy Spirit reveals to me…

Day 312

Emotional unplugging is a coping mechanism that blocks your receptivity of Holy Spirit's guidance.

#stopblocking

In the Emotions of my identity, Holy Spirit reveals to me…

Day 313

If you're still thinking it's someone else's fault, you're still forgetting the purpose of emotions. How long are you going to settle for that?

#stopit

In the Emotions of my identity, Holy Spirit reveals to me…

Day 314

If you feel unsettled about it, it's because you know it's unsupportive of moving you into alignment with God's Will for you.

#youknow

In the Emotions of my identity, Holy Spirit reveals to me…

Day 315

When you realize you're choosing to be emotionally triggered, you find the free-will moment to choose a different response.

#choosedifferent

In the Emotions of my identity, Holy Spirit reveals to me…

Day 316

The moment you accept that you chose your own struggle is the moment you become empowered to slay it. You are a Struggle Slayer!

#slay

In the Emotions of my identity, Holy Spirit reveals to me…

Day 317

Anxious thoughts remain active in you when your prayer life is non-existent.

#prayconstantly

In the Emotions of my identity, Holy Spirit reveals to me…

Day 318

It's amazing! The more the Art of Living Grateful is pursued, the more life becomes great and full.

#livinggrateful

In the Emotions of my identity, Holy Spirit reveals to me...

CHAPTER 12: BEHAVIOR

TURN YOUR EYES UPON JESUS
LOOK FULL IN HIS WONDERFUL FACE
AND THE THINGS OF EARTH
WILL GROW STRANGELY DIM
IN THE LIGHT OF
HIS GLORY AND GRACE.

HIS WORD SHALL NOT
FAIL YOU HE PROMISED
BELIEVE HIM AND ALL WILL BE WELL
THEN GO TO A WORLD THAT IS DYING
HIS PERFECT SALVATION TO TELL.

~ 'Turn Your Eyes Upon Jesus'
by Helen H. Lemmel

Day 319

It is ALWAYS about the choices you make.

#always

In the Behavior of my identity, Holy Spirit reveals to me…

Day 320

Stop waiting for the light at the end of the tunnel. Light it up yourself.

#belight

In the Behavior of my identity, Holy Spirit reveals to me...

Day 321

Speak your heart, it's calling you to your Jesus family. You are held and lovingly supported.

#hearttruth

In the Behavior of my identity, Holy Spirit reveals to me…

Day 322

Relentlessly honor your God-nature. Give it space to rise. Study your whole self and become an expert in how you were created.

#godnature

In the Behavior of my identity, Holy Spirit reveals to me...

Day 323

Find cause in sorrow. Gather strength from discomfort. Grow brave by trusting you were created to receive guidance from Holy Spirit.

#receiveguidance

In the Behavior of my identity, Holy Spirit reveals to me…

Day 324

Stay in your lane. Serve from the heart. Be passionate about your earth-life purpose.

#heartpassion

In the Behavior of my identity, Holy Spirit reveals to me…

Day 325

Take ownership of where you're going next and how you're going to experience it.

#takeownership

In the Behavior of my identity, Holy Spirit reveals to me…

Day 326

Make your choices today as if God gave you free-will.

#freewill

In the Behavior of my identity, Holy Spirit reveals to me…

Day 327

Invest yourself in being human, the way Jesus modeled. Activate those supernatural skills!

#supernaturalskills

In the Behavior of my identity, Holy Spirit reveals to me…

Day 328

Your most resourceful choice is to behold Holy Spirit 's guidance. So you can go beyond, whatever you thought is holding you back.

#beholdtogobeyond

In the Behavior of my identity, Holy Spirit reveals to me…

Day 329

Sometimes it's what you must UNbelieve.

#releaseit

In the Behavior of my identity, Holy Spirit reveals to me…

Day 330

Honor what is most self loving, the way Jesus loves you. What you gain is vital, what you lose is nonessential.

#selfloving

In the Behavior of my identity, Holy Spirit reveals to me…

Day 331

The YOU that Holy Spirit has been teaching, you're THAT person now. Live from there.

#livefromthere

In the Behavior of my identity, Holy Spirit reveals to me…

Day 332

It's time to step into that big bold vision God gave you.

#itstime

In the Behavior of my identity, Holy Spirit reveals to me…

Day 333

10 THINGS TO CUT OFF:

1) Self-doubt.
2) Inaction.
3) Regrets.
4) Bad Relationships.
5) Mindless Choices.
6) Indifference.
7) People Pleasing.
8) Reactivity.
9) Bad Health.
10) Mean Self-Talk.

In the Behavior of my identity, Holy Spirit reveals to me…

Day 334

Make your life a "Negative-Self-Image-Free" zone.

#negativityfreezone

In the Behavior of my identity, Holy Spirit reveals to me...

Day 335

Be pro-awareness and anti-indifference.

#bepro

In the Behavior of my identity, Holy Spirit reveals to me…

Day 336

Refuse to get sucked into the manipulation. Remember it's all just an illusion.

#justillusion

In the Behavior of my identity, Holy Spirit reveals to me…

Day 337

Activate vulnerability with yourself, it exposes where you need alignment with Jesus.

#alignment

In the Behavior of my identity, Holy Spirit reveals to me…

Day 338

You've been repeating a hard lesson to fulfill a purpose you haven't achieved. This time...last one, best one!

#bestone

In the Behavior of my identity, Holy Spirit reveals to me...

Day 339

Master non-duality and BE...easy like Sunday morning.

#beeasy

In the Behavior of my identity, Holy Spirit reveals to me…

Day 340

Your outcome is the way you are BEing. If you don't like the outcome, change the way you are BEing.

#belikejesus

In the Behavior of my identity, Holy Spirit reveals to me…

Day 341

Nurture your body, starve your negative self-image.

#nurture

In the Behavior of my identity, Holy Spirit reveals to me…

Day 342

A world-class Extension of God's Love is one who edifies the awareness of God's image in others.

#edifygodinothers

In the Behavior of my identity, Holy Spirit reveals to me…

Day 343

You're a grown-up human. Stop using the same thinking program from when you were a child. Run the program you need for when you are now.

#yougrownup

In the Behavior of my identity, Holy Spirit reveals to me…

Day 344

How you role model your Human Identity is dependent on the influence of your Spirit Identity.

#rolemodel

In the Behavior of my identity, Holy Spirit reveals to me…

Day 345

Make your Soul shine with the brightest brilliance so you illuminate the path for others.

#illuminate

In the Behavior of my identity, Holy Spirit reveals to me…

Day 346

Blaze a trail that can be celebrated by dancing angels in Heaven!

#dancingangels

In the Behavior of my identity, Holy Spirit reveals to me…

Day 347

Allowing what's outside to be inside will only hold you down. Empower what's inside to dump what belongs outside.

#empower

In the Behavior of my identity, Holy Spirit reveals to me…

Day 348

The best way to spend a life is by creating a zero-regrets legacy that outlasts it.

#zeroregrets

In the Behavior of my identity, Holy Spirit reveals to me…

Day 349

You're blazing trails! Get off your butt, get on your feet, and set your world on fire for Jesus!

#firetrails

In the Behavior of my identity, Holy Spirit reveals to me…

Day 350

Respond to everything from a place of knowing who you are.

#knowyou

In the Behavior of my identity, Holy Spirit reveals to me…

Day 351

You chose them to be in your life. Model ambition to; remember their true identity, manage their mind, own their outcomes, and live empowered experiences.

#modelambition

In the Behavior of my identity, Holy Spirit reveals to me…

Day 352

Challenge yourself to level up one new gratitude more.

#newgratitude

In the Behavior of my identity, Holy Spirit reveals to me…

Day 353

Encourage yourself to leverage your emotions by; observing them, taking responsibility for them, and learning what Holy Spirit is teaching you from them.

#leverageemotions

In the Behavior of my identity, Holy Spirit reveals to me…

Day 354

Live each moment to discover your next most-aligned choice. It's ok if others don't get it...you're doing it right.

#mostaligned

In the Behavior of my identity, Holy Spirit reveals to me...

Day 355

Make your head space, heart space, and hustle space a negativity-free zone. Only good vibes allowed.

#goodvibes

In the Behavior of my identity, Holy Spirit reveals to me…

Day 356

Make choices as if this is the moment you found your first love...Jesus.

#firstlove

In the Behavior of my identity, Holy Spirit reveals to me...

Day 357

Look for and find in other people's desires the perspective you need for you to follow yours.

#perspective

In the Behavior of my identity, Holy Spirit reveals to me…

Day 358

You know that negative self-speak you sometimes have? Just stop it.

#now

In the Behavior of my identity, Holy Spirit reveals to me…

Day 359

Honor your integrity over your ego and...feel right about it.

#honorintegrity

In the Behavior of my identity, Holy Spirit reveals to me...

Day 360

Positively impact lives while you're here and also plant seeds of positive impact for when you're gone.

#seedsofpositivity

In the Behavior of my identity, Holy Spirit reveals to me...

Day 361

It's your mission to relentlessly pursue awareness of your Spirit Identity so that others will relentlessly pursue awareness of their Spirit Identity.

#relentlesslypursue

In the Behavior of my identity, Holy Spirit reveals to me…

Day 362

You either decide to set your mind to focus on the things of God or you choose to leave it as an open field for developing devilish deeds.

#focusongod

In the Behavior of my identity, Holy Spirit reveals to me…

Day 363

Don't pursue or desire luck...Seek Jesus who holds the keys and opens doors.

#seekjesus

In the Behavior of my identity, Holy Spirit reveals to me…

Day 364

True and sobering fact, you are only here for a brief moment in time. Prepare for Eternity now.

#eternitynow

In the Behavior of my identity, Holy Spirit reveals to me…

Day 365

Live a lifestyle of loving with gratitude, not anger with baditude.

#gratitudevsbaditude

In the Behavior of my identity, Holy Spirit reveals to me…

ABOUT JESUS CENTRIC MIND MINISTRIES

VISION

In a ministry setting, train and equip individuals and couples with transformation tools to mature the parts of your mind that are unresourcefully conditioned and ready to be advanced, according to the guidance of Holy Spirit.

MISSION

In-person/virtual proven and highly successful, transformative trainings for personal growth and skill building where the tools are learned and practiced under the mentoring of Jesus Centric Mind Ministries trainers.

PURPOSE

Graduates of Jesus Centric Mind courses use these tools for yourself and to help others live empowered from your Spirit Identity with a Jesus Centric Mind in all areas of life, as Jesus modeled.

JESUS CENTRIC MIND MINISTRIES

jesuscentricmind.com

a ministry of

NET-WORKS CHURCH LAGUNA BEACH

lagunabeachnet-works.org

ABOUT THE AUTHORS

Jason E. Lohrke

- 1988 Christian Rock Band Ministry
  - Asight Unseen
- YWAM International Missions
- 1994 Vanguard University
  - Pastoral Ministries B.A.
- 1997 VCC Church Planting
- Youth/College Pastor
- Relational Pastoral Counseling
- Substance Abuse Ministry
- Sexual Addiction Ministry
- Inner Healing Prayer Ministry
- Worship Leader
- Singer-Songwriter
- Immanuel Prayer Facilitator

Paula Higa Lohrke-Moyer

- 1989 Christian Rock Band Ministry
  - Asight Unseen
- YWAM International Missions
- Home Educator - 9 years
- NLP Trainer and Master Practitioner
- Master Life & Success High Performance Coach
- International Speaker and Coach - 31 years:
  - Education, Health & Fitness, Personal Growth Life & Success, High Performance (mindset)
- Trainer - 12 years:
  - Business, Fitness, Professional Certifications Neuro-Linguistic Programming (science of renewing the mind)
- Transformation Curriculum Writer
- Transformation Trainings Designer
- Immanuel Prayer Facilitator

www.ingramcontent.com/pod-product-compliance
Lightning Source LLC
LaVergne TN
LVHW020652110826

845149LV00012B/1966

9798989783106